Gemma Hoy is a new author who is brutal but honest in her writing. She has spent her career managing pubs and working in education, where she served as a Head of Mathematics and Lead Practitioner of Mathematics in secondary schools. She has now transitioned into adult education and has found time to take up new hobbies, including writing. She exclusively writes about subjects where she has personal experience and aims to put a comedic perspective on events, whilst not ignoring the serious messages of certain situations or topics.

In loving memory of:

Robert E. Harris
Robert Oldcorn
Ravinda Singh
Mark Robert Richardson
Vicky
Bryan

And all those who have lost their lives to this eternal battle.

Gemma Hoy

# BLOW ZERO

AUSTIN MACAULEY PUBLISHERS
LONDON · CAMBRIDGE · NEW YORK · SHARJAH

Copyright © Gemma Hoy 2025

The right of Gemma Hoy to be identified as author of this work has been asserted by the author in accordance with sections 77 and 78 of the Copyright, Designs and Patents Act 1988.

All rights reserved. No part of this publication may be reproduced, stored in a retrieval system, or transmitted in any form or by any means, electronic, mechanical, photocopying, recording, or otherwise, without the prior permission of the publishers.

Any person who commits any unauthorised act in relation to this publication may be liable to criminal prosecution and civil claims for damages.

The story, experiences, and words are the author's alone.

A CIP catalogue record for this title is available from the British Library.

ISBN 9781035894307 (Paperback)
ISBN 9781035894314 (ePub e-book)

www.austinmacauley.com

First Published 2025
Austin Macauley Publishers Ltd®
1 Canada Square
Canary Wharf
London
E14 5AA

Thank you to UKAT and all of their staff who took the time to care and understand.

Thank you all for being my friends and for the impact you have had on my life and the lives of others.

Good luck and best wishes to anyone who is reading this. Thank you for taking the time to do so. You are valuable, you are worthy, and you matter.

Gem
x

# Foreword

This book is dedicated to Robert E Harris. He was the inspiration for this book and began writing it himself but was told the characters were too unbelievable. However, every anecdote in this book is true! Robert E Harris wrote three books himself, and I strongly encourage you to look them up, especially if you enjoy this one. He made many mistakes in his life, but he lived and loved. We should all love each other at some point. There is always a place for forgiveness. This book will be both funny and devastating at times—but unfortunately, that is the reality of life. The main characters are Gemma and Danni, with Rav, Robert, and Mark also playing important roles.

# Introductions

In this first chapter, I will introduce you to the main characters of our story. Firstly, there is Danni, a talented artist living in Liverpool. Secondly, there is Gemma, a Head of Maths based in Barnsley. Next, there is Mark, a self-made businessperson from Scotland. Then there is Robert, an Economics professor at the University of Liverpool, and finally Rav, an Asian Cockney geezer who, despite all his bravado, was terrified of women! As you can tell, these five people had very little in common on the surface, but the one thing they all shared was what society might call a drinking problem. Now, I despise this term, mainly because it makes no literal sense. These guys did not have a problem with drink; they bloody loved it! In fact, I would go as far as to say they were professionals. I am not just talking about people who go over the top on a Friday night—I am talking about people who, if drinking were an Olympic sport, would take home the gold every day. (Unless they were competing against each other, in which case the event would last longer than a test match in cricket, and there would definitely be some ashes at the end). Anyway, I digress. This book is not about making light of a serious illness—far from it. In fact, if you are reading this and you have an addiction problem, please know that whilst recovery is hard, it need not be scary or shameful. You might just end up meeting some of the nicest people you have ever met in your life!

# Chapter 1
# Arrivals

Really, I should leave this chapter blank for Rav, Robert, and Mark because none of them had a clue what was happening on day one. The same could be said for the next five days for the boys! Gem and Danni, however, had decided not to drink before their arrival, and that leads me to explain the title of the book. When you first arrive at a rehab centre, you will be breathalysed. Gem and Danni both blew zero. I know you are probably thinking, "Good on Gem and Danni," but they had a more controversial reaction. When the nurse said, "We do advise that people have a drink before they come in for medical reasons," Danni's response was, "Can I go out for a few hours and come back again?" Gemma's response was simply, "Motherfucker!" Meanwhile, the boys were all over the place. Mark was demanding white wine; Robert looked like a cross between Freddy Mercury and an extra from *Shameless*, and Rav thought the lift was his bedroom. Nevertheless, they all managed to make it to the smoking shelter, walking down a slope in a line—the five of them looking like the usual suspects, except they were all Keyser Söze before he lost his limp!

This is where our story truly begins. This book will consist of 27 more chapters, each one detailing the events of a different day in rehab. Please enjoy, and if you have found anything offensive so far, I suggest you stop reading pretty swiftly!

# Chapter 2
# Socialising

I have called this chapter "Socialising" because that is what each of our usual suspects attempted to do, though on CCTV it looked more like some kind of nature programme where a bunch of pandas are put together, and all they do is stare at each other and occasionally roll down a hill! By this time, Gem and Danni had already shared their disappointment at not realising they should have had a drink before coming in. However, they were feeling slightly smug, having realised that because they had been sober, they were given the good drugs (Librium) much sooner than the boys!

The first thing that happened on day two was COVID tests. This led to the first conversation between Gemma and Rav. When I say conversation, it was more a shared hilarity over another patient who attempted to take a COVID test by putting the swab up his nose and then into his mouth, effectively deep-throating his own snot! Rav simply said to Gemma, "Shall we tell him?" to which Gemma replied, "Nah!" Meanwhile, Mark had finally had his first dose of Librium and, after claiming it did nothing, tried to get up from a seat situated rather close to a wall and ended up headbutting the brickwork. Gemma and Danni found this scenario so hilarious that they proceeded to fall off their chairs themselves!

Robert, by this time, had made himself relatively presentable—apart from his Freddy Mercury moustache—but had forgotten his cufflinks and decided to fashion some out of wool! Danni had started sketching (producing extremely impressive work). She wanted to paint but wasn't allowed the materials in case she sniffed them. The most notable thing about this day was that it was a Sunday. For food, our five were presented with a self-service roast dinner. Everyone agreed there was nothing wrong with the food, but they had to question the appropriateness of giving five people with the shakes the task of serving up hot gravy. Robert's white shirt was not going to survive that one! So, covered in gravy, suffering minor burns, and trying desperately to eat peas with a fork without them all falling off, they began to bond.

# Chapter 3
# Groups

When day three hit, everyone decided they were fit enough to join in group sessions, which they would continue for six hours a day for the next twenty-six days. The group sessions varied; some were what were called "process groups," where everyone would share how they were feeling that particular morning. Others were "life stories" or step work, the details of which I will not share for obvious reasons. At the start of the process group, everyone in attendance was requested to share a word to describe how they were feeling that day. Rav chose the word "fine." The way the therapist reacted, you would have thought he had said, "I feel like shitting on your nan's chest." Apparently, there is no right or wrong answer when expressing your feelings, but this therapist had other ideas and insisted that "fine" was not a word that should be used in group sessions. Robert and Mark were confused and started doubting what they had come to know as the English language, and after a long debate about whether or not the word "fine" was indeed fine to use, Gemma and Danni thought their heads were going to explode. They were no longer content, excellent, first-class, satisfactory, or copasetic. The five swiftly learnt that the best way to get along smoothly in these process groups was to read a thesaurus the night before. After all, the words "exceptional," "exquisite," and "refined" were all deemed to be acceptable—or, in other words, they were fine.

# Chapter 4
# Bowel Trouble

By this time, the Librium was kicking in, and each of our crew was feeling the results on their respective digestive systems. Being woken up at 6.30am for a dose of Librium isn't the worst thing in the world—unless you have been up all night on the toilet. Danni described her "troubles" as being like having tiny little rabbit droppings: pointless but constant. Mark said that he sat there for forty minutes at a time, trying to push what felt like a watermelon out of him. Gemma compared her movements to Hiroshima, while Rav and Robert looked on in disbelief at the conversation. The most notable thing about *this* day was when Gemma was on the toilet. She made such a noise that a workman outside her room thought his colleague was shouting to get his attention! The hilarity of this situation was so overwhelming that Gemma ran outside to tell Danni all the details. The urgency with which Gem approached Danni made poor Danni think something was urgently wrong, but no—Gemma was quite literally talking shit. There is nothing quite as funny as hearing someone say, "What was that, mate?" just after you have emptied your bowels! So, there you go. Only day four, and already our five are sharing—the start of some beautiful friendships.

# Chapter 5
# The Injection Stories

What I didn't mention earlier was that, from day one, our five were subjected to vitamin injections called Pabrinex. Apparently, celebrities pay good money for these, and according to the nurse, our characters were getting them for free. She must not have been in the office when they passed over a total of £50,000 between them for a month's stay in a single room.

The injections were exceedingly painful, and the nurse's ability to administer them was questionable. There were definitely residents who would have been more skilled at injecting. The boys decided that the pain wasn't worth the outcome of having great nails and soft hair, whereas Gem and Danni were made of stronger stuff! Mark and Rav claimed that, without having any hair in the first place, there was very little point, while Robert simply exclaimed, "I have had a prick in my arse before, and it didn't hurt nearly as much as those injections!"

Gem and Danni had a different attitude, but both were wondering if it was more painful to have a prick in their arse or a prick in their lives, and decided that both situations were equally as painful.

# Chapter 6
# The Alarm

It was a wonderful day in rehab when the fire alarm went off, by which I mean everyone was outside enjoying the sun. Rav was on his phone, having finally been able to use it now that his hands had stopped shaking and he was no longer in danger of knocking his teeth out. Danni was still sketching with a pencil that she was only allowed to sharpen under supervision. Gemma was probably on the toilet, and Mark and Robert were becoming wonderful friends, having discovered that they both shared the same name. After, on day one, Mark had drunkenly pinged Robert's braces and declared that his name was also Robert, despite having introduced himself as Mark. (He, of course, meant his middle name but didn't elaborate on this fact for a few days!)

It may seem like a fire alarm going off is a minor thing, but of course, there are always protocols to be followed. Quite typically, there was a meeting point where everyone needed to gather and be accounted for—nothing unusual there. What was unusual was that the fire warden instructed all the patients to walk through the building to get to the meeting point, despite the fact that they were already outside. Not only that, but there was also a side gate at the bottom of the grounds that would have allowed them access to the meeting point! The irony of the fact that the group, for once in their lives, wanted to take the safe option was lost on this fire marshal. Just to top off the illogical nature of this entire situation, whilst standing there huddled like a group of confused penguins, the group witnessed one of the therapists deciding that, in the midst of a potential life-threatening situation, surrounded by addicts, she would light up a cigarette! Keith would definitely have had something to say about that day!

# Chapter 7
# The Suitcase Contents

When you first come into a rehab, you have no idea what to expect, so most people try to second-guess exactly what they will need for the month. Of course, that sounds like a simple task, but not when you are under the influence, or 'off your tits,' if you will. It's almost like planning to go on holiday, but instead of a feeling of excitement, you have a sense of impending doom. After a week, things had become a lot clearer for our five, and they began to properly unpack their suitcases. The reality of the state they had all been in before entering the centre became clear, and they all decided to share stories about what they had discovered in their suitcases.

Robert had neatly folded identical shirts, braces, and corduroy trousers, which he intended to wash and wear for the rest of the month, despite the heatwave. Rav had packed a very questionable object that looked like a wind chime but took another two weeks to identify as a religious relic. Mark had packed quite well (as someone else did it for him), but unfortunately, all his T-shirts had some sort of alcohol-related promotion on them. Gemma had also packed relatively well, but in addition to her normal clothes, she discovered a wetsuit and a single flip–flop. Finally, Danni had packed what, a week previously, could have been identified as fruit. The reality of the effects of alcohol on the brain was more paramount than ever, and there is actually a very serious message here: Do not pack your own suitcase before entering a rehab centre!

This would be an appropriate time to explain the fact that any electronic devices, such as phones, iPads, hair dryers, etc., were taken out of the suitcases when they were searched on entry to the centre. These were put in a locker that could be accessed between 7pm and 9pm each day, and 3pm until 9pm on weekends. Unfortunately, when Mark first arrived, he had forgotten that his phone had been taken away from him and spent at least four days looking for it! Gemma, on the other hand, was extremely sneaky. She took two phones in, having had some previous inside information that all technology would be restricted. She therefore signed out her unusable old iPhone every evening and weekend, so as not to raise suspicion, but kept her current phone in the lining of her suitcase! A small crime, but the girl's talent for getting what she wanted was undeniable, especially when she smiled politely and charmed every member of staff into thinking she was sweet and innocent. (That couldn't be further from the truth!)

So, having unpacked and laughed at each other's misfortunes (although no one knew about Gemma's phone until they all left—she wasn't silly enough to risk losing it by telling anyone), the group resigned themselves to the fact that perhaps they were not quite as compos mentis whilst drinking as they all thought they were!

# Chapter 8
# The Orders

It probably goes without saying that residents were not permitted to leave the premises unsupervised, so there was no opportunity to stock up on cigarettes, treats, etc., by physically visiting a shop. However, a month is far too long for anyone to be expected to go without some sort of pleasure, so Tuesdays and Fridays became what came to be known as 'Snappy Shopper' days. If anyone is looking to open a local convenience store, I recommend that you do so near a rehab centre, because twice a week you will be in receipt of the orders of forty or so addicts who have swapped their drug of choice for an addiction to Doritos, cigarettes, and Jelly Babies. Snappy Shopper is an app much like Deliveroo, where the user can connect to a local shop and order anything that shop stocks to be delivered. Gemma, Danni, Mark, and Rav acted like it was Christmas every time Tuesday or Friday came around. Robert, on the other hand, was less bothered. He was heard to say, "My body is a temple," after he had 'borrowed' his fifth cigarette in an hour from Mark and had eaten nearly half of Gemma's Haribo. It was a shocking realisation to behold just how much cigarettes cost when buying them in bulk, especially when our five were smoking more than London in the 17th century.

What was nice about these days was the ability of all of our residents to share and look out for each other. You would think that people would resemble Gollum in *Lord of the Rings* once they received their order, but nothing could be further from the truth, apart from on one occasion when someone decided to take Rav's chilled can of Coke out of the fridge and nearly had their head put through a window. But you can understand his frustration.

Another funny thing that happened one 'Snappy Day' was when Gem decided that she would whisper something to a fellow resident called Matt. What Gem wanted to tell him was that she had ordered him a vape and she didn't want any of the other residents to hear. Unfortunately for Gem, she had forgotten that Matt had a condition called deafness, so whispering in his ear had very little effect. Not knowing the volume of his own voice, Matt simply exclaimed, "What are you doing? I'm fucking deaf, mate!"

This routine of purchasing soon became the norm, and every one of our characters had a drawer dedicated to treats and supplies. Each and every one of them were now highly skilled in stock taking and rationing, being able to surmise how much they needed to order on each occasion to keep them going until the next 'Snappy' day. Addiction clearly had some valuable transferable skills.

# Chapter 9
# Meds

There was a strict schedule for medication that applied to all residents in the rehab centre. Meds were taken at 6.30am, 12pm, 4pm, and 9pm. Not everyone needed medication at all of these times, but the majority had their own medication to take in addition to what was prescribed by the doctor at the centre.

If you attend a rehab clinic, on arrival, after you have sat on the end of your bed for a while trying to figure out exactly how you got there in the first place and where life went wrong, you will have a Zoom meeting with a doctor. He will ask you how much you drink on a regular basis and prescribe a dose of Librium accordingly. It is generally in an addict's nature to lie about how much of a particular substance they consume, and, on this occasion, Rav made that exact mistake. Gemma, Danni, Mark, and Rob, however, went in the opposite direction, quickly realising that the more extreme the problem was, the greater the dosage of Librium they would receive.

When 6.30am came on the second day, all of our five were sat precariously on chairs outside the medication room, tearing skin from their own fingers, waiting for what they had now come to realise was a rather good substitute for alcohol.

Gem, Danni, Mark, and Robert were all given nine tablets, which quickly took effect and saw them all laughing giddily at their horror toilet stories from the night before. Rav, on the other hand, having pretended to be an evangelical misunderstood individual who only ever overdid things on occasions, was given three tablets. Not only was Rav by far the heaviest drinker of them all, but he was also six foot five and built like a brick shit house, so the Librium had about as much effect as a Tic Tac for him.

While the other four were merrily enjoying laughing at their own shadows, Rav was vomiting over the side of the wall and had to rely on Gem and Danni to help him rectify the situation. Against his own instinct, he was finally honest about the quantity and type of alcohol he consumed and subsequently joined the others in their hazy but enjoyable morning.

# Chapter 10
# Step Work

As previously mentioned, details of individual step work will not be shared in this book, but I will share the process. Each of our five were booked in for a month, so each were required to complete a 'life story,' a 'step one,' and a 'step two.' The life story process is quite self-explanatory, but the step one and step two required a little bit of reading and a show of understanding of the process.

In simple terms, the step one is about admitting a problem, and the step two is about thinking about how to change things. Of our five, Gem, Rob, and Danni were the most academic and, therefore, the most confident writers. Not that Rav and Mark didn't have impressive talents, but they weren't, shall we say, patient when it came to writing long statements. As a result, Mark decided to ask Gem to help him with each step, something that was encouraged by the staff, so long as both individuals were comfortable with it. Gem had absolutely no problem with this, as being a teacher, it was her forte to help others with things that they found difficult.

She did not, however, appreciate the fact that it became apparent that she was not helping Mark; he was simply copying everything she was writing down without even paying any attention to the content. I have previously described Gemma as sneaky, but cunning more accurately describes her in this situation. Noticing that Mark was copying her work, she decided to write down an answer in the hope that he would blindly copy it without taking in any of the detail. She therefore came up with a cunning plan!

In response to the question, "What are you grateful for today?" Gem wrote down, "I am grateful that my smear test came back negative and that my pregnancy scare is no longer apparent." Sure enough, Mark began to write down this answer word for word, and as the realisation came across his face, Gemma fell off her chair laughing. Never again would Mark take advantage of Gemma, and from that point on, he admired her subtle ability to punish complacency in the most unique way!

Despite having identical questions and similar answers, all five of them approached these tasks in slightly different ways and followed the same process of being productively challenged by a therapist on their answers once they had read them out. This was an exhausting and gruelling process that required a lot of honesty, thought, and soul searching. All were pleasantly surprised that they did, in fact, have a soul, but were left exhausted and emotionally drained after each step, having realised what bastards they had all been at some points in their lives.

The most interesting thing that came out of all their step work was the similarities they all shared in relation to addiction. From buying birthday cards to make the shop owner think that the fancy bottle of gin was a gift for someone, to buying cocktail sausages to create the impression that they were having a party with the quantity of alcohol they were buying, they had all done it. Apart from Rav, who didn't give a shit what anyone thought of him, least of all a stranger in a shop.

# Chapter 11
# Newbies

After about a week or so in rehab, it had begun to feel like home for our five. They had all unpacked, made friends, learnt the routines, and finally taken back control of their bowel movements (or at least adapted to them). As you can imagine, most days someone would leave the centre having completed their stay, and someone new would arrive. The comradery really shone through when new people arrived, as every single person who was residing in the centre—whether they had been there for a day, a week, or a month—appreciated how unnerving it was on day one.

Different people had different attitudes when they arrived: some hid away in their rooms for a few days, some were straight out trying to meet people, and some were still so hammered they had no idea where they were. I'll correct that last statement—MOST had no idea where the hell they were. Danni referred to the Newbies as Bambis because, when trying to walk, they looked like they were trying and failing to ice skate. But there was never any judgement, just a shared experience, and everyone tried to make someone who had just been admitted feel as welcome and as comfortable as possible.

Having been there for a while, our five started to think of themselves as veterans and would willingly and enthusiastically help people to find their way and learn routines. There are a few events that happened with new arrivals that really stick out, and I will document them here now, having changed names for anonymity purposes.

Firstly, there was Elle. Danni, Gem, and Mark first met Elle outside the medication room at 9pm on her second day. Having found her confidence, Elle walked around the corner in her dressing gown and shower cap (for some unknown reason) and exclaimed, "Morning, guys." Gem and Danni looked at each other with an expression that simply said, "Who is going to tell her?" before Mark piped up and said, "Elle, it's 9pm." She struggled to live that one down for the rest of her stay, especially as shortly after, she attempted to sit down and completely missed the chair!

Next, there was Debs, who came outside as soon as she arrived. Suffering with the inevitable shakes, she attempted to light a cigarette, narrowly avoiding her hair and eyebrows. When realising that she was about to vomit, she put her lit fag out in Mark's coffee. Again, there was absolutely no ill feeling or judgement, and Robert and Mark offered to help her to her room. Deb's room was upstairs, so they decided to take the lift. Debs stood outside the lift doors, patiently waiting but swaying like she was on a boat in the middle of a tsunami. When the lift arrived, she announced, "Thanks, guys, I'm here now," and walked back outside without going upstairs.

There was also Sally, a middle-aged primary school teacher who arrived on a Sunday. Sally had the same problems that Rav, Robert, Gemma, Danni, and Mark had had at the start of their stay—in the fact that shaky hands and gravy are not a good mix. To add insult to injury—or should that be injury to injury—Sally was wearing shorts when trying to pour her hot gravy and ended up looking like she had made some sort of dirty protest.

Lastly, there was Ethan, who perhaps made the most dramatic entrance of anyone. Ethan had been to this rehab centre before, so was well known by the staff, but obviously not the fellow residents. He began his stay by wanting to introduce himself to everyone, and when I say introduce, there wasn't much left to the imagination. The staff knew very well that he was a perfectly lovely person who wouldn't hurt a fly, but that was very difficult for a stranger to recognise at this stage of his stay. Ethan didn't look dissimilar to a 1940s gangster, so he was not the most approachable person on first impressions, especially when he began diving all over the women, fell down the hill, and declared that he was going to have sex with every single female in there.

As little as two hours later, Ethan reappeared with absolutely no recollection of what he had said and done. Gem was sat by herself in the kitchen completing some work when he came and asked to sit next to her. Rav, Robert, and Mark looked on in horror, expecting some sort of Incredible Hulk moment from Gem as she had been less than impressed by his previous behaviour, but she was so flabbergasted by the rapid change in persona, she actually thought he was a completely different person! In the end, everyone took great pleasure in letting Ethan know exactly what had happened a mere two hours before, and he apologised profusely, especially to Gem, whom he told had the right to give him complete shit for the rest of his stay. A statement he quickly regretted making!

# Chapter 12
# Heat Waves, Hot Food, and Hospitals

This period of time this book is written about refers to May – June 2023, which saw a huge heat wave in the UK. This was lovely for all of our residents because, when they weren't in group therapy sessions, they were able to relax and/or socialise in the grounds of the centre. As it was so hot, it began to become customary for the men to want to remove their shirts, and, guaranteed, just as they did, a member of staff would appear demanding they put them back on. The ladies found themselves in a similar situation, often being chastised for wearing too little. When asked why this was, a lot of the staff were cagey and refused to answer, but one member of staff revealed that it was because there were sex addicts amongst the crew. When this revelation was made, the gang resembled a group of people playing a murder mystery game—all looking at each other suspiciously. The only exception to this was Robert, who sat at the bench in his nearly full suit, observing the activities in the grounds. I'll just leave that there and let you make your own conclusions.

Despite the hot weather, the kitchen had a strictly regimental menu and would not be flexible with this in any sense of the word. Robert had perhaps the most unfortunate incident with a cook when he knocked on the kitchen door and overheard one of the kitchen staff say, "What the fuck does he want now!" To this day, he is still not quite sure why he in particular was so unpopular with the kitchen staff!

Pretty much everyone wanted to have something cold to eat on these hot days, but as was previously mentioned, the menu was the menu, and there was no adapting to it. So, unless all forty of our residents suddenly developed allergies, they were stuck eating curry and roast dinners in thirty-degree heat. No one particularly enjoyed this, especially as the curry had, as Rav put it, meat that was as chewy as Ghandi's flip flop and sauce that had less taste than watered-down baked beans. The adverse consequences on the guts go without saying, but there were also some serious repercussions, as three residents actually collapsed after being in the sun all day and eaten curry at 5pm. (There was also no flexibility on mealtimes).

This was clearly not a funny situation, and three separate ambulances were eventually called, requiring three separate members of staff to leave the premises in order to escort each individual to a hospital. The knock-on effect of this was that agency members of staff were then called in to cover those who were offsite. Now, I'm no mathematician, but I imagine the cost of three ambulances and three members of staff's wages might just outdo the cost of swapping a curry for a salad. Logic and safety both took a big hit that day, and this time, not from the residents!

# Chapter 13
# The Evenings

After around 6pm, structured time finished, and the residents were free to do as they pleased. (Well, not exactly as they pleased, as we all know how that would have ended up!) Some decided to watch a movie, some played a board game, or, as the weather was so nice and the nights were light, a lot decided to stay outside and just chat. On a few occasions, someone would suggest a film, and a group would gather in one of the communal lounges to watch it. It was difficult to pick a film that everyone liked, so generally, a film was picked that everyone disliked in equal measures. These were commonly horror movies.

One rare evening, Danni, Gem, Rav, Rob, and Mark, having had enough of the sun, decided to go upstairs and join in the watching of a film called *The Conjuring*. None of them were particularly keen on horror movies, but they thought they would give it a go. The premise of the film is one of a typical horror: a family moves into a haunted house, and someone becomes possessed by a demon. However, this film seemed to have the ability to make all of our five jump out of their skin. This was the first time they discovered that the numbness caused by alcohol was beginning to fade away.

(Not the ideal way to make that discovery). I think they lasted about twenty minutes before Rav looked like a waxwork model un able to move through shock, Mark was holding his heart, Robert was questioning the plot but also whether or not he could ever look at a doll in the same way again, Gem had spilt tea everywhere after claiming she wasn't clumsy, and Danni ran out of the room and vowed never to turn the light off ever again.

A more popular pastime in the evening was to spend time outside enjoying the warm evenings and the nicotine. This is where it was normally possible to find any or all of our five characters. Some of the stories they shared during these times could take up an entire book themselves, but I will recall the funniest from each one of them, starting with Rav.

Rav had Indian heritage but was very much born and bred in London, which became apparent as soon as he opened his mouth. He did, however, use his heritage to his advantage on more than one occasion, most notably when he was stopped for speeding by the police. In response to the officer's question, "Do you know how fast you were going?" he described how he nodded and answered "No" at the same time and then proceeded to answer "Yes" and shake his head. He then told how he repeatedly said the phrase "Very little English" in a strong Indian accent. As Rav had planned, the officer then let him go on his way, to which Rav responded, "Cheers, mate!"

Robert's story was less controversial legally, and on first impressions, one would not have expected it from the man. But after a few days of knowing him, his anecdote came as no surprise to anyone. Robert recalled several occasions where he would frequent brothels. Gemma found this particularly amusing when she asked what he used to wear, and he simply pointed to his white shirt and corduroy trousers. This, however, was only part of the tale. The most notable event that happened was when Robert was found hiding in a bush in a stranger's front garden in a full suit having accidently mixed legally prescribed drugs with alcohol during an evening out.

Gemma's story involved a festival and a tattoo—a recipe for disaster before we even start! When attending Reading Festival one year, Gemma and her friends arrived at the arena from the campsite just as the bars were opening. Having enjoyed a breakfast of bacon and cider, they were ready for the day. As they were early, they visited the Bacardi tent and were confronted by the bar manager, who said that if the girls delivered some flyers for him, they could have a free drink. They swiftly accepted this offer, but Gemma jokingly said, "If I go to that tattoo tent next door and get a Bacardi bat tattoo, can I have free drinks all weekend?" The bar manager, probably not expecting to hear any more about it, agreed to the deal. Gemma, being gifted with the skill of being able to complete mental mathematical calculations quickly, took no time to deduce that this was financially the best option and visited the tattoo tent that morning. She therefore received as many five-pound Bacardi cocktails as she wanted that weekend, having only spent thirty pounds on the tattoo, and has since vowed never to touch or smell the stuff again, despite the remaining ink.

Mark's story also began when he was much younger and on holiday in Greece. Whilst on a catamaran, he had taken advantage of all-you-can-drink booze cruise, and while the rest of the passengers were enjoying seeing dolphins and whales in their natural habitat—a once-in-a-lifetime experience—Mark was busy hanging over the edge, adding to the natural make-up of the Atlantic Ocean with cheap regurgitated Spanish beer and tapas.

Danni's story relates to her time in Liverpool, where she lived as a student and managed to make it home at 4am one morning. Well, at least she thought she did. In fact, she walked into completely the wrong halls of residence and laid in the bed of a complete stranger, only to be woken up to the rest of the flat staring over her. In her hungover state, she still did not realise that she was in the wrong place and simply rolled over and went back to sleep.

As you can imagine, there were plenty more stories that emerged throughout the month, but these seem to best represent the individual character and mentality of each of our five.

# Chapter 14
# The Meetings

Days in rehab have a rigid structure, and the schedule for every day began with a peer meeting in the morning at 8.30am after everyone had had a chance to have their healthy breakfast of a coffee and a cigarette. This meeting was a chance to welcome newcomers, say goodbye to people who were leaving, and go through any issues or questions. At the start of each meeting, every member of the group was required to introduce themselves, make reference to their addiction, and say how many days they had been clean for. Despite them all coming in on the same day, Robert, Mark, and Rav were always two days behind Danni and Gemma because it took them that long to lose the alcohol from their systems. But nevertheless, it began to be quite a therapeutic process.

At this point, I will need to refer to another resident named Phil, who took it upon himself to list every single addiction he had. From trainers to Branston pickle, the poor lad was addicted to everything and may have finally come to the realisation that he was also addicted to rehabs!

The second type of meeting that took place was a community meeting. These meetings were more formal and involved all members of staff, including the kitchen staff, so Phil was more reluctant to admit his addiction to general household items and food products and stuck with the traditional cocaine and alcohol.

Gem, Robert, Mark, Rav, and Danni despised these meetings as they seemed to descend into chaos with people talking over each other and not listening to anything anyone else said. The whole process resembled a day in the House of Commons. In fact, our five did great impersonations of politicians during this hour. Danni fell asleep, Robert and Mark nodded along politely pretending to respect what was being said but were actually screaming inside. Gemma walked out, stating she had had enough of all the bullshit, and Rav saw this as his cue to follow her in protest.

The types of 'discussions' that took place were, in our five's opinions, not worth having. After all, who really cares if Sandra forgot to put her spoon away for the twelfth time? Sandra has been using the same spoon at home for a year, although that might not have been for the purposes of eating a yoghurt.

# Chapter 15
# The Boss

Every rehab centre has what is called a business manager, who is not a therapist or a member of the medical team, but oversees the finances and general running of the centre. The main qualifications you would need to have to pursue this kind of career are absolutely no social skills and an inability to listen or show any empathy or respect to anyone, including your own members of staff. In this chapter, I will take the time to describe 'The Boss' and let you draw your own conclusions.

Let's start with our five's first encounters with 'The Boss'. Gemma met him first in the most unfortunate of circumstances. As we will explore in another chapter, on arrival to rehab, clients are buddied up with another resident who has been there for a longer period of time in order to make them comfortable and give them a point of contact should they have any questions. One morning, Gem was walking down the corridor, and Rav said to her, "Gemma, have you seen our new resident? They want you to be his Buddy." Not thinking any more of it, Gemma went up to who she thought was a new resident and offered to show him around, kindly opening with the line, "Hi, I'm Gemma, I'll show you around if you would like me to. Don't worry about still being drunk, most people are when they first arrive."

The Boss' already red face went purple with rage, and Gemma soon realised Rav had intentionally fooled her into thinking the Boss was a fellow addict. The thing that gave it away was when he responded, "I am in charge of this centre, and I don't appreciate your joke." Most people would have seen the funny side to this, but he most certainly did not, and from that point on, he was not a fan of Gemma.

Danni, Mark, and Robert found this story most amusing, and so did Gemma after she had got over the embarrassment of being fooled. But in her defence, the Boss did bear an uncanny resemblance to Father Christmas (after he had been all around the world and drunk the cheap free brandy that people left out for him).

# Chapter 16
# The Buddies

In a previous chapter, I referred to the Buddy system that required one resident to buddy up with a new resident in order to make sure they knew what they were doing in their first few days at the centre. All of our five both had buddies initially and became buddies later on. As they all had very little memory of the first few days, there is not a lot to say about their experiences of having a buddy, other than the fact that Mark's buddy could not tell him where he could get white wine from and Rav's buddy did not enjoy the experience of having to explain for the fifth time that the lift doors were not his bedroom doors. Their experiences of *being* buddies, however, are worth commenting on.

Mark was asked to buddy up with a man called Alex, a security guard from Newcastle. Alex arrived at the centre expecting something more luxurious than what he was presented with, and from that point on, he was not entirely happy. When deciding to admit himself to the centre, he read what he referred to as a brochure and was under the impression he would be staying in a lovely country house. Unfortunately, he did not look up the postcode and failed to realise he had booked into a refurbished old people's home in the middle of a council estate in Barnsley. When Mark approached him and offered to show him around, he simply replied, "I'm not interested in any of that shit," and retired to his room. It was actually not unusual for people to act in this manner when they first arrived, and later on in his stay, Alex regaled some humorous anecdotes of his time as a security guard, the most notable of which being when his pet Chihuahua chewed through a vest designed to withstand bullets and machetes.

Danni was asked to buddy Emma, a young girl who was in the middle of her university degree. Danni did not get on with Emma, the main problem being that she was completely barmy and not in the cute adoring way that Gem and Danni were. Emma's parents had booked her into a rehab centre, seemingly with a caring intention, but probably just to get rid of her for a month. That seems like a harsh sentence, but this girl would run around the grounds in the rain, stand pretending to be a scarecrow for hours, and stay up all night singing "Rehab" by Amy Winehouse. The irony of the lyrics may seem funny in retrospect, but at 5am it was very much the opposite.

Rav was asked to show Mohammed around. The staff made a completely random and non-biased decision when asking Rav to buddy up with Mo, who really appreciated Rav's attention to detail and commitment to the job. Rav showed outstanding efficiency when he handed Mo a form and said, "Hi, I'm Rav, sign this form that says I have shown you everything that you need to know."

Gemma and Robert's experiences of being buddies were less remarkable, perhaps because they were both educators, used to dealing with anxious people whose brains were not working correctly, or perhaps because they were partnered with like-minded people who were equally as eccentric, and they just didn't notice. Either way, everyone tried their best (Rav really did try his best – his actions were polite for him!), and each of the new recruits soon settled in and became part of the gang.

# Chapter 17
# The Team Leaders

In order for the peer group to have a democratic influence on the running of the centre, every week they elected two team leaders who would represent the rest of the peers and be the link between the staff and the residents. As they say, with great power comes great responsibility, and when Gemma and a fellow resident called Niel were elected to be team leaders, they were initially flattered. This, however, lasted about an hour before they wanted to rip their own eyeballs out.

The trouble with being team leader is that you become a sounding board for everyone's grievances, and a group of forty addicts detoxing after years of abusing their bodies are not the easiest group of people to manage. The staff prided themselves in the fact that they allowed the peer group to have a say in the day-to-day running of the centre, or at least that's what they told the residents. In reality, someone came up with the wise idea of allowing the residents to elect representatives in order to create the illusion that they had some power when really all the staff wanted was someone inoffensive who could deal with all the bullshit arguments that they didn't want to hear about.

There was one incident that will haunt Gemma and Neil for the rest of their days. As team leaders, they would introduce themselves to people who were new and offer to help them out if needed. One evening, Gem and Niel were watching a film with some fellow peers when there was a knock at the door. It was Richard, an elderly gentleman who was clearly a little bit lost and confused, but recognised Gem and Neil, sat down on the sofa next to them and said, "Oh, I'm glad I've found you, I need your help." They were more than happy to help until Richard exclaimed, "I've just shit myself." Gemma's eyes went wide, and Neil's jaw dropped. Both looked at each other in disbelief at what they had just heard. Gemma froze, but Neil sprang into action and walked behind Richard to check his pyjama bottoms.

"I can't see anything," he kindly declared before Richard responded, "I know, it's on my bed." This was beyond their pay grade, so Gem and Neil went to request help from a member of staff before vowing never to sit on that part of the sofa again.

# Chapter 18
# The Smoking Shelter

With the weather being nice, most of the residents smoked in the grounds but were only really supposed to be smoking in the designated smoking area. This wooden structure with a bench that sat six was a genius design intended to safely accommodate all forty of our smokers. For some reason, the smoking shelter seemed to be where all the fun happened. It was almost like being at school behind the bike sheds, where all the things happened that were not supposed to happen.

One evening, just as it was getting dark, Gem, Danni, Mark, Robert, and Rav were sat at the bench chatting away when Phil came along to join them. Just as Phil turned up, two of the therapists were leaving in a car that was parked on the other side of the fence. It wasn't possible to see through the fence completely, but it was possible to make out shapes and hear. Phil did not seem to realise that the therapists were talking through the fence; he was under the impression that the tall cylindrical cigarette bin was some sort of communication device and began to speak into the holes at the top. Once again, hilarity ensued, and Phil was now capable of declaring that he was addicted to talking to used cigarette ash.

# Chapter 19
# The Second Boss and the Ipad Incident

One day, during the morning meeting, just after Phil had shared the details of his new addiction to pillows, an unexpected event occurred. The lead therapist entered the room and announced that she had some news: the boss had left his position. The shock and grief amongst the staff lasted an entire eight seconds, and later that day the residents were introduced to their new commander and chief: Adam. Adam was the polar opposite to the first boss with regards to looks and attitude, but he most definitely possessed the same vital skills necessary for the position. The lack of social skills and general disregard for anyone else's feelings was particularly strong in this man. The main difference between Adam and our first boss was the attitude he had towards Gemma. This, however, did not start on day one; there is a story behind it that Adam would probably rather forget.

In the staff office, there were a series of iPads for staff to use for various purposes. Adam needed to film some CCTV footage from the main terminal, and he therefore grabbed the nearest iPad, pressed record without unlocking it, and filmed

CCTV footage of a serious medical emergency that had occurred in the building the night before (when there were no qualified medical staff on the premises, but that's another story). Having recorded the footage, Adam thought he would have a look at the quality of it on the iPad before sending it to head office. It was here that he struck a problem, as he was unable to open the iPad. Concerned but not yet panicking, he turned to his trusty colleague Katie, who had more than just Key Stage One computing under her belt, and asked her to help him open the iPad. Katie could not open the iPad because it was not an iPad that belonged to the centre; it was Gemma's iPad that she had dropped off in the office after signing it out of her locker for a work meeting.

Adam was horrified and asked Katie what he should do, to which she responded, "There is not a lot you can do, you will have to tell Gemma what has happened."

For the next half an hour, our 'man of the people' Adam tried to figure out who Gemma was, and after mistaking five different people for her, he finally found her. Gem is not the type of person who would want to get someone into trouble for a stupid but honest mistake, so she promised to keep the events a secret, but was fully aware of the position of power she had just obtained. She deleted the videos and kept her word. The next day, Adam came rushing up to Gemma again, sweating profusely and shouting, "What about the cloud, what about the cloud?" It seemed to come as a shock to Adam that Gem hadn't let two videos left on her iPad consume all her thoughts in the previous twenty-four hours, but she soon realised that he was referring to the iCloud and a wry smile appeared upon her face. She calmly and confidently said, "This is about my recovery, not yours, Adam," and went on her way. After this point, Gem could have sniffed cocaine off a full bottle of vodka whilst taking ketamine, and Adam wouldn't have blinked an eyelid. She had him wrapped around her little finger, and didn't he know it. She did not do anything with the information and never would, but the remaining days went pretty smoothly for her.

# Chapter 20
# Cheese Gate

Despite our crew all getting on relatively well, there were some inevitable tensions that occurred in the midst of a group of forty recovering addicts living in a small environment. The most memorable occasion involved their collective newfound addiction to cheese. Having paid a small fortune to stay in this establishment, it could be reasonably suggested that all of our crew could make some small demands of the kitchen. This, however, was not the attitude of the kitchen staff or management.

In order to explain this part of the story properly, I will first need to point out the fact that there was a toastie maker in the communal kitchen free for anyone to use, but unfortunately, unless you wanted to toast your own clothes, face, or hands, there were limited options as to the use of the aforementioned appliance.

Robert was the first to request cheese from the kitchen, which was a big mistake. He was greeted with the traditional "what the fuck does he want now" response from the kitchen staff before being told that the kitchen budget did not stretch to cheese. Confused and disillusioned that his £10,000 didn't stretch to allowing him to have cheese, he decided to share his experience with the group. The following scene somewhat replicated the Cinicinnati riots of 1829, except this time, Irish immigrants and native blacks were not after jobs; they were after cheese.

It is (or should be) pretty much common knowledge that if you deny an addict of anything, they will want it more and find a way to get it. Before you knew it, the cocaine addicts were snorting parmesan, the alcoholics were eating brie while drinking cranberry juice, and the heroin addicts were injecting primula spread. Where they got it all from, we will never know, but these guys always find a way!

# Chapter 21
# Football Crazy

It was a strange time in rehab when the play-off finals started. Cov City had a chance to get to the Premier League; they were playing Luton Town. On a serious note, Gem had tickets to Wembley that day, but she made the decision not to go, in order to allow herself to take the time to attempt to make herself better. Cov lost on pens, and Luton were promoted to the Premier League. I do not know if you have ever been to Luton's ground, but you pretty much need to walk through a back garden to get there. It made Rochdale away look like Buckingham Palace.

The next day, Barnsley were playing at Wembley in the play-off finals for League One. That did not go well either! Gem wasn't alone in having tickets for Wembley that weekend. A fellow resident, Jay, had tickets to go to see his beloved Barnsley. Both were loyal fans of their respective teams and were somewhat devastated for themselves and for each other. However, for the first time in as long as they could both remember, they did not feel like reaching for the bottle. Both had about fifty coffees and ninety cigarettes over a period of forty-eight hours and congratulated each other on how healthy and sensible they had been.

# Chapter 22
# Another New Customer

On day twenty-two, a somewhat strange character entered our establishment. Dave had what some might refer to as a questionable past, or at least he said he did. Dave lived as a traveller, or in more realistic terms, someone who called themselves a traveller but never actually moved unless he was being chased by the police.

On day one, Dave was very willing to tell the tale of how he had been shot twice, but this story didn't quite add up in Gemma's mind. (Mainly because she had been sober for almost a month, and her brain almost worked properly again). As normal, our five welcomed Dave and tried to make him feel comfortable, but there was always something that didn't sit quite right about him.

When he eventually managed to travel to his first group session, he unfortunately decided to challenge Gemma for no reason at all. Now, Gemma is quite an amenable individual, but as has been previously mentioned, she has the ability to be quite assertive. On this one occasion when Dave decided he would challenge our Gem, he did travel. He travelled back to his room and was never to be seen again. Bless him. Gem never boasts about what she can do, but she is clearly capable.

So, having taken two bullets, our Dave couldn't cope with a head of maths from Barnsley and her friends.

# Chapter 23
# Yoga and Gong

This chapter will be difficult to write, mainly because our five weren't aware of what yoga and Gong involved. However, they all partook and left very confused. Yoga is quite a common thing to do, but again, a questionable exercise to give a group of people with precarious balance. Gong is not as usual as Yoga, and it is a very strange concept to think that smashing a hammer on a massive bell would help people sleep, but it did! I think the infusion of incense and the confidence of Danni and Gem passing out straight away helped everyone else to sleep. Gem also took great pleasure in sleeping next to Ste, someone who she found marginally attractive to say the least.

The only problem anyone had during this session was with Dan's snoring. She was harmonising with another person and didn't have any awareness, but according to all reports, she is a beautiful sleeper. I, however, disagree. The sound of a pig getting murdered is far more accurate.

Yoga was a little less relaxing, and it probably goes without saying that having good balance and posture is not something any of our residents practiced on a regular basis. They did, however, display excellent breathing techniques when they all resembled a block of dominoes, collapsing in a heap, suffering minor injuries and a few serious cases of winding and flatulence.

# Chapter 24
# Ethan's Piles

Ethan was mentioned once before in this book, and he probably deserves to be mentioned more, mainly because he wasn't just one man, he was three: him, himself, and his piles. The poor guy was in agony, but considering his entrance, Gem had limited sympathy with him, especially after he had said that Gem had permission to treat him in any way she wanted to. (Ethan had no idea how strong of a woman Gem was, but he was about to find out!) Gemma is a nice person, but her sense of humour is slightly deranged. The day started out with Gem making sure all the bald men had sun cream on their heads. Unfortunately for Ethan, this turned out to be quite an ordeal. Giving Gem permission to do anything she wanted meant that, whilst applying sun cream, she was rather vigorous (by which I mean, she slapped it on his head and told him to shut the fuck up with his moaning!). Poor Ethan had an extra two balls hanging out of his arse and now looked like someone was going to cue off with him. At least he didn't ever pot the black.

# Chapter 25
# The Music Therapy

Music Therapy was a somewhat difficult time, mainly because music and therapy should not be in the same terms. You play music, and you have therapy. What you readers must understand at this point is that a lot of alcoholics are also very literal people, so the confusion that they suffer is over the level of understanding for what society would call normal people. On this day, our crew all had to choose a song that they wanted to hear and explain why they wanted to hear it. Danni chose 'Smack My Bitch Up' for reasons she would share in her own time. Gem chose 'Wake Me Up When September Ends' because she had nearly been in rehab for a month. Robert chose 'Bohemian Rhapsody' by Queen because he is one and also fancied wasting ten minutes of everyone's time. Mark chose 'Return to Sender' because he had an amazon delivery package on his mind, and Rav chose 'Walk Like an Egyptian' because he was still suffering minor spasms in his arms, which made one stretch out forwards and the other backwards! I'm not entirely sure this is what the therapist had in mind when she said, "Choose a song and explain why you chose it." Perhaps a better term would have been 'Choose a song and explain what it means to you.' There is a subtle difference between the two requests, but as previously mentioned, a lot of addicts are very literal people, so they took the original request slightly differently than it was intended.

# Chapter 26
# Anxiety

With only two days left to go, our group started to realise that the outside world did actually still exist, and whilst the smoking shelter had seemed like home for 24 days, it was not possible to live there indefinitely. Anxiety about any new event is common for people, but when the new event involves people and places that have already been seen, this anxiety is heightened. It may seem confusing to say that going into the outside world was a new event, but it was in the sense that the world can change a lot in a month and people can change a lot in rehab. The anxiety presented itself in a lot of different forms, but the most obvious one was the self-questioning. Danni was worried that she wouldn't have the inspiration to draw any more if she was sober. Gem worried that she wouldn't have the same charisma. Mark worried that he would go back to a huge empty house without the dogs that he loved. Rob worried that he would be too stressed out without alcohol to look after his mother, who he cared about dearly, and Rav worried that without drinking he wouldn't gamble and would therefore have no way of getting any money! All of these thoughts may seem insane, but addiction and insanity are like a married couple that have been together for 40 years. They know they are no good for each other, but they just can't be apart. Unfortunately, addiction and insanity go hand in hand, and this terrible illness does not just stop. An addict could have had two days sober or two years sober, but will still remain an addict. The life sentence our five had attained was beginning to become apparent.

# Chapter 27
# The Last Night

I will now write in the first person to reveal that I am Gemma and have been writing this book partly to help myself, but also in the hope of helping others.

On day twenty-seven, we all knew we were going the next day, but it was terrifying. We tried to have a good night, but we were all so scared. This is not an exaggeration. When you have been in a rehab centre for nearly a month, things start to not be as funny as they were at the end of week one. We had told the honest truth about everything, and I think it struck us hard. The outside world is not the kindest to people, and some of the memories brought about by sharing so deeply in a safe environment made it seem all the more terrifying. We all still needed help but were all still more willing to help other people than ourselves. Every addict that I have ever known is a loving person. In my experience, she or he would go out of their way to do anything for anyone. Most of us have done no intentional harm to anyone apart from to ourselves, but the knock-on effect of any addiction on family and loved ones is indescribable. Addicts could be artists, doctors, teachers, technicians—the list is endless. We love and accept, and that is the only thing we have in common apart from addiction.

But it's the best thing to have in common, and a trait that is not as usual as it should be in 'normal' society.

# Chapter 28
# Goodbyes

It was a difficult and somewhat sad day on day twenty-eight for us. Despite the emotionally draining nature of meetings and courses, the realisation that the outside world was waiting for us had finally kicked in. Being in a safe environment for a month and then entering the big wide world again is a daunting experience, and didn't we all know it. I think, given half the chance, we would have all stayed and reminisced about stories of cheese, madness, recuperation, and quite frankly, a fun and sober time. Nevertheless, it was time to say our goodbyes and depart. The morning meeting on this particular day was a reminder that we had only started our journey to recover from this horrible illness. It is all well and good being sober for a month in a controlled environment, but continuing that in the outside world is somewhat harder. However, we had learnt a lot, laughed a lot, and loved a lot, and that was something that we would carry with us for the rest of our lives.

# Chapter 29
# Finale – A Series of Unfortunate Events

This final chapter is a short but completely serious one. Having left rehab and gone our separate ways, all of us stayed in touch, but felt somewhat lost. The bonds developed in one of these places are like no other, and in one month, we knew more about each other than we did about friends and family that had been in our lives for years. There was a sense of pure trust and comradery, and each of us continued to enjoy chatting and sharing with each other in a way we could not with anyone else. Danni and I met up a few times, and bizarrely, Danni's mother ended up taking care of my cats when I moved house and remains their carer to this day. I would not have trusted my animals with most people, but I had faith in the friendship I shared with Danni and therefore trusted that they would be safe in her mother's care. Robert went back to working as a well-respected professor at the University of Liverpool, and Rav moved back to London, taking up a new flat where he could be away from previous stresses.

Mark and I had struck up such a bond that one day, Mark asked if I wanted to visit him in Telford, which I did, and we didn't look back. We lived together happily in Mark's house, reminiscing and creating new memories, watching rubbish TV, and helping each other to recover. Both of us said it was the best time of our lives, and we laughed every day. Unfortunately, in April 2024, Mark was admitted to hospital and suffered a cardiac arrest from which he never recovered. He lived a fantastic life and brought up three fantastic children. Equally as sadly, Rav was admitted to hospital with stomach pains and also passed away with his children and nephew by his side. Both will be fondly remembered by many, and this book is written in their honour. Rest in peace, Rav and Mark. Two beautiful souls taken too soon.

There is also something I need to address; Robert E Harris, to whom this book is dedicated, was in a lot of pain when he finally passed away. Unfortunately, the term "died peacefully" is one that I don't think should be overused because the majority of the time people panic and are in pain. Robert E Harris called me and told me that he was trying to come to terms with things and that it was all over. I didn't accept it at the time, and am still struggling to, but he, like my other two boys, died, and there were terrible songs played at his funeral. What he would have wanted was the Pet Shop Boys – "You Were Always on My Mind." I think, with his mentality, it applied to everyone he knew.

Robert – You are always on my mind.
Mark – You are always on my mind.
Rav – You are always on my mind.